SCIENCE FOR LIFE AND LIVING
INTEGRATING SCIENCE, TECHNOLOGY, AND HEALTH

Order and Organization

BSCS *Innovative Science Education*
founded 1958

KENDALL/HUNT PUBLISHING COMPANY
2460 Kerper Boulevard P.O. Box 539 Dubuque, Iowa 52004-0539

Acknowledgments begin on page 197.

ISBN 0–8403–5990–X

This material is based on work supported by the National Science Foundation under grant No. MDR-8652131, the Adolph Coors Foundation of Colorado, the Gates Foundation of Colorado, and IBM Educational Systems of Atlanta, Georgia. Any opinions, findings, and conclusions or recommendations expressed in this publication are those of the author(s) and do not necessarily reflect the views of the granting agencies.

IMPORTANT: Please be advised that use of *Science for Life and Living* requires goggles. Students will use a variety of common objects and materials (for example, rubber bands, hammers, and screwdrivers, and household chemicals such as vinegar) whose use requires eye protection. Standardized safety goggles are required to be used with *Science for Life and Living* as indicated in the program, without exception.

iii

CONTENTS

UNIT
1

Introduction to the Year's Themes

ORDER AND ORGANIZATION

Teams

Team Skills

Move into your teams quickly and quietly.

Speak softly.

Stay with your teams.

4

Take turns.

Do your jobs.

Team Jobs

The manager gets and returns supplies.

The communicator may ask the teacher for help.

The communicator may ask another communicator for help.

Teams do things.

Teams talk about things.

Teams learn, and teams have fun!

Left or Right Thumb?

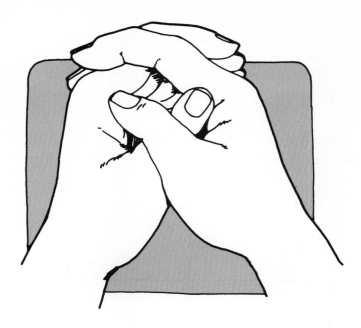

Dear Family,

In science class, your child is learning about <u>sorting</u> as a way to organize things. The students sorted themselves in many ways. One way they sorted was by observing which thumb was on top when they folded their hands. The class found that some people felt more comfortable with the right thumb on top; others put the left thumb on top. The class recorded the results.

Please help your child with an assignment by doing the same hand-folding experiment. Your child will record the results and begin to organize information. Please follow these directions:

1. Fold your hands. (Your child can show you how.)
2. Tell your child which thumb is on top.
3. Let your child trace your top thumb onto the Family Record Page on the back of this letter.
4. Repeat this exercise for everyone in the family. Be sure to include your child.
5. When you have finished, ask your child to show you how the record helps to organize the people in <u>one</u> family into <u>two</u> groups. (Maybe the results of the experiment will leave your family in <u>one</u> group.)
6. Send the Family Record Page to school with your child tomorrow or the next day.

Thank you for your help.

Sincerely yours,

Your child's teacher

Family Record Page

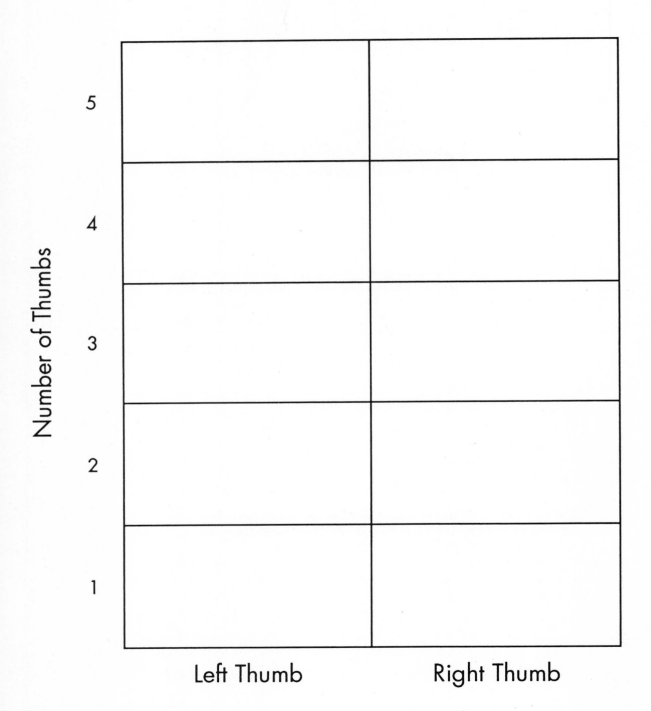

Sorting

Sorting People

How could you sort these people into two groups?

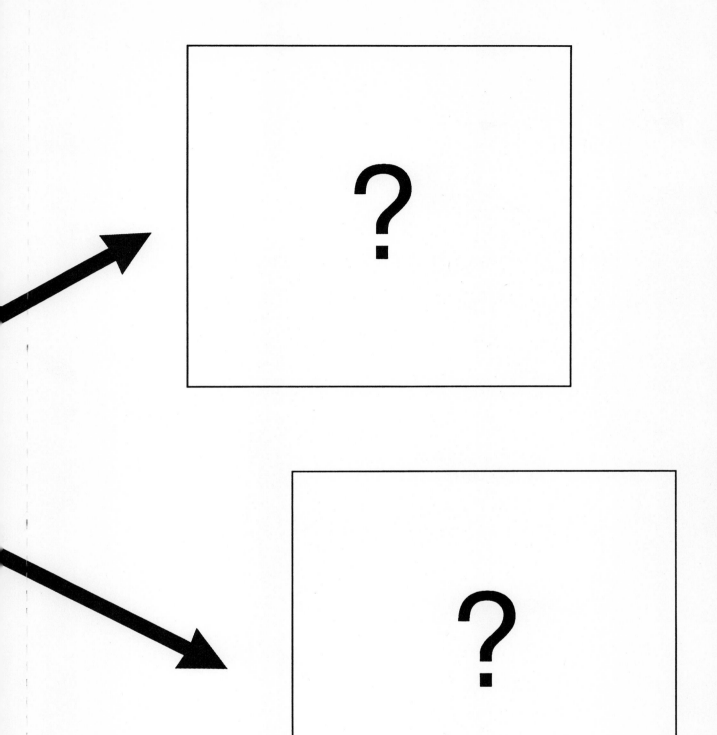

Magnet Mystery

Sorting Objects

How could you sort these objects into two groups?

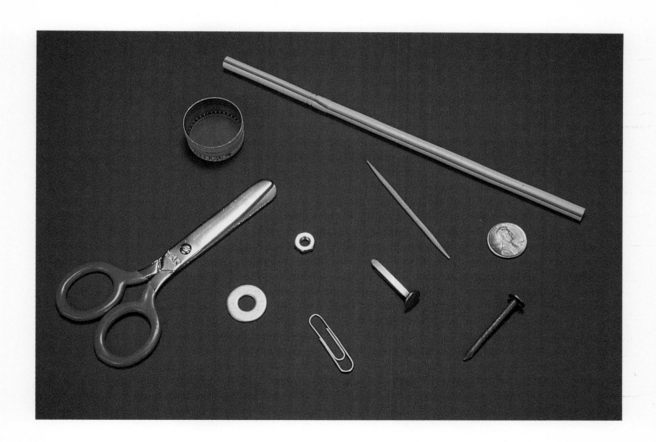

Does It Stick To the Magnet?

Circle Yes or No.

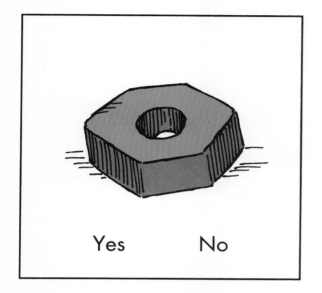

Yes   No

Yes   No

Yes   No

Yes   No

Name _____

Name _____

Does It Stick To the Magnet?

Circle Yes or No.

Yes   No

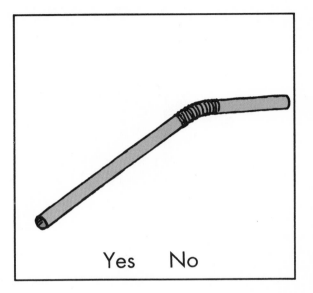

Yes   No

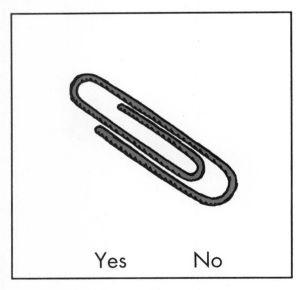

Yes   No

Yes   No

Name _____

Name _____

What Have You Done?

Sorting Pictures

How could you sort these pictures into two groups?

What Have You Done?

What Have You Done?

Sorting

You sorted people into groups.

You sorted objects, too.

Sorting is a way to organize things.

What other things can you organize?

UNIT 2

Objects and Properties

ORDER AND ORGANIZATION IN SCIENCE

Gloop

Observe with your senses.

Taste only food.

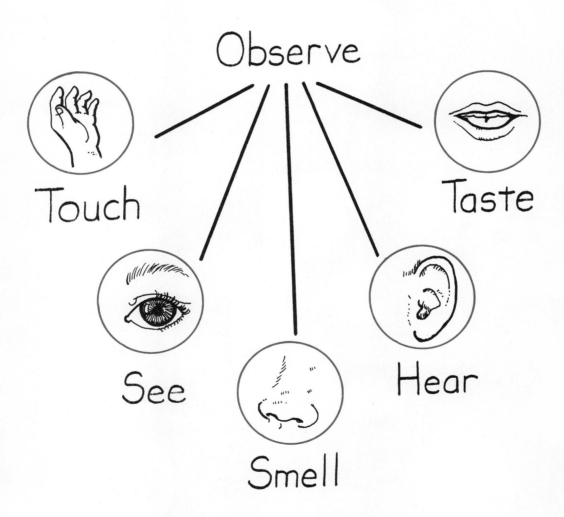

Observe to find out about things.

Team Skill

Share the things you use.

Gloop

Observe to find properties.

Properties of Gloop

Write words that tell about gloop.

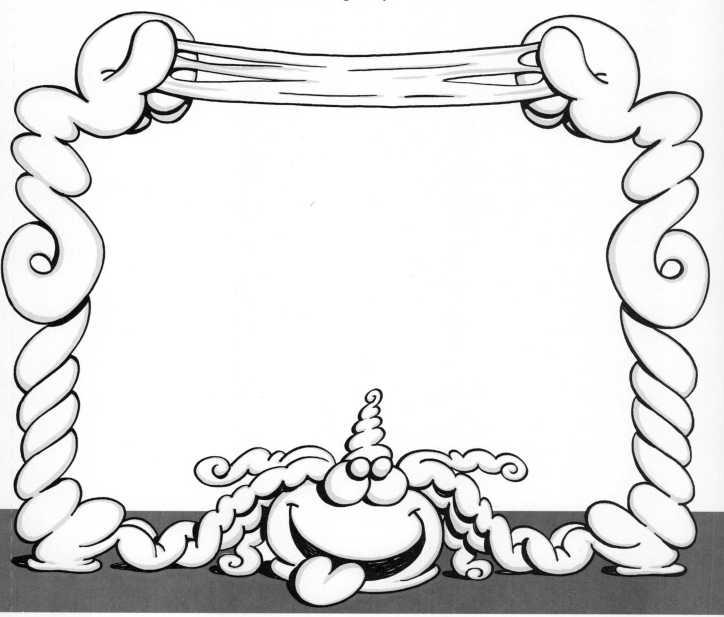

_____ and _____
(name)   (name)

Let's Sort Leaves

Fall leaves—
Shuffle through a bunch!
Leaves rustle,
and crackle,
and crunch.

Properties of Leaves

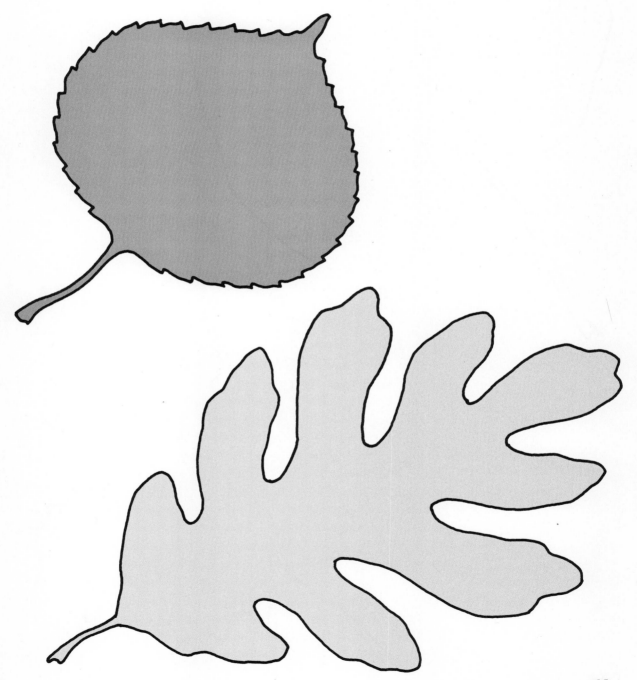

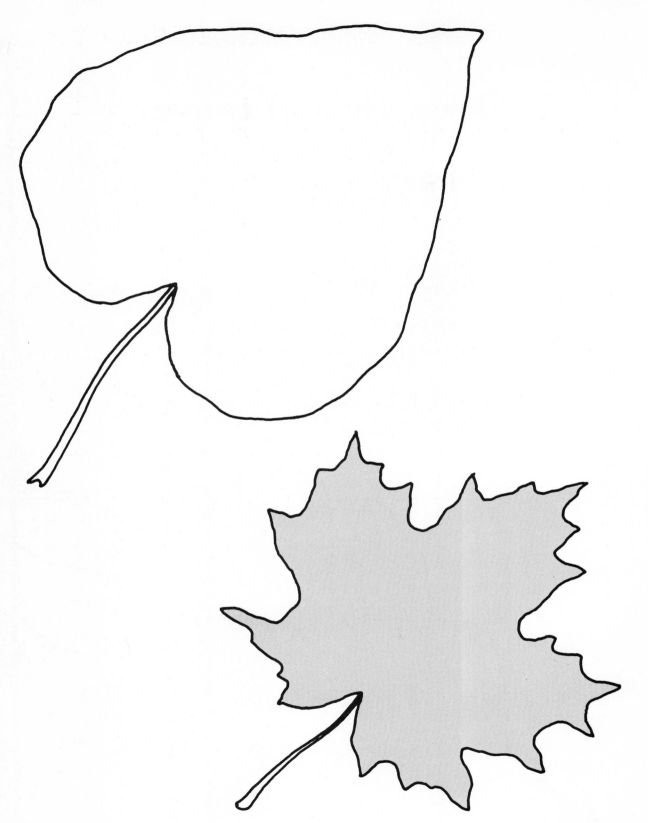

I See a Sequence

Size is a property of objects.

Size is a property of people.

Name _____

 # Short to Tall

Draw everyone in your family.

Shortest	In Between	Tallest

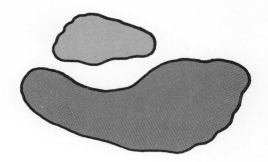

Dear Family,

We have been sorting objects into groups according to properties. Size is one property of objects. We are learning to arrange objects in a sequence according to their size. We will arrange outlines of feet in a sequence.

Today, my partner and I traced our feet. We want to put the outlines of our feet in a sequence from short to long. We need more outlines of feet. So, tonight I have some homework. I am going to trace one foot (shoe off) of each member of my family. I brought home paper to make the outlines. After tracing a foot, I will need to cut out the outline and write the person's name on it.

I will try to do as much of my homework as I can, but if I ask for help, will you please help me?

Thank you,

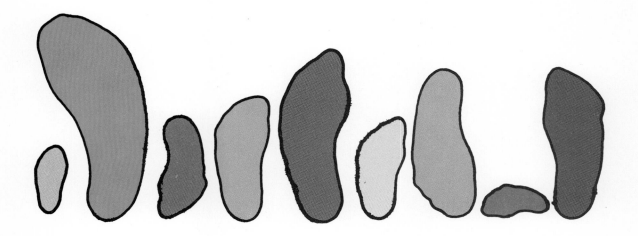

Shoe Store

How could you organize these shoes?

Shoe Sizes

Tomorrow, our class will
sort our shoes by size.

I need to find out my shoe size.

My shoe size is

Name _____

My Size

I found out my shoe size by

_____ kids wear my size!

Trying on Shoes

These shoes are no prize,

They can't be my size!

cause they crunch,

and they scrunch,

and they jab, pinch, and poke!

My poor mashed, smashed feet,

Think these shoes are a joke!

Put This Room in Order!

CRASH! BANG! Jung Soo groaned and stuck her head under her pillow. "It's that noisy garbage truck," she thought. Finally, the crashing and banging stopped. Jung Soo smiled as she snuggled down to sleep.

R-R-R-OAR! Jung Soo sprang straight up
in bed. "That train!" she thought. Jung
Soo put her head under her pillow again.
HONK! HONK! Jung Soo moaned. "Why
didn't those trucks beep instead of
HONK," she thought.

"I'm so tired. I can't sleep with all
these CRASHES and BANGS and ROARS."

Jung Soo thought about why she was so tired. Her four cousins had come over to visit last night. What fun they'd had in her room! Her room? That reminded Jung Soo of something. She pulled down the covers and peeked out from under her pillow.

What a mess! What a terrible, horrible, mixed-up mess! Nothing was where it was supposed to be. Jung Soo sat up. She put her elbows on her knees and her chin on her hands. What would her sister say when she came home from spending the night at her friend's house?

Just then, there was a knock on Jung Soo's door. "Come in," she called.

Jung Soo's mother poked her head into the room and gasped. "What on earth happened to your room?" she asked.

Jung Soo looked around the room.
Then, she looked at her mother. "Well,"
she sighed, "I was sound asleep in my
nice, neat room. Then, a three-story-tall
giant looked in my window. He winked at
me and laughed. Then, he picked up my
whole room and shook it very hard. He
shook it four times! Didn't you hear the
crashing and banging? I was so scared
that I put my head under my pillow."

Jung Soo's mother looked at Jung Soo. She looked all around the room. Then, she said, "Yes, I <u>did</u> hear a crashing and banging. You must have been very frightened. It's too bad that the noisy giant didn't stay and help you put this room in order. Now, you will have to do it all by yourself! When you finish, come and have breakfast." Jung Soo's mother shut the bedroom door and went away.

"GROWL!" Jung Soo's stomach sounded like her cousin's puppy. She was very hungry, but her mother told her to put her room in order <u>before</u> she came to breakfast. Jung Soo started to get out of bed, but there was not one empty space on the floor for her to stand.

Just then, someone knocked on the door. Jung Soo called, "Come in." Jung Soo's grandfather poked his head in the door, looked around, and shook his head back and forth.

"What on earth happened to your room?" he asked.

Jung Soo looked around the room.
Then, she looked at her grandfather.
"Well," she sighed, "I was sound asleep
in my nice, neat room. Then, a tornado
whirled in my window. It whirled all
around my room, scattering stuff
everywhere. See what a mess the tornado
made? Didn't you hear the thundering
roar? I was so scared that I put my covers
over my head!"

Jung Soo's grandfather looked at Jung Soo. He looked all around the room. Then, he said, "Yes, I <u>did</u> hear a roar. You must have been very frightened! It's too bad that the tornado didn't whirl around some more and help you put this room in order. Now, you have to do it all by yourself! After you put your room in order and eat your breakfast, you can go to the library with me to check out new books." Jung Soo's grandfather shut the door and went away.

Jung Soo was so hungry that her stomach felt like an empty balloon. Just then, someone knocked on the door. Jung Soo said, "Come in."

Jung Soo's brother, Woo Jong, poked his head in the room, looked around, and whistled. "What on earth happened to your room?" he asked. Jung Soo looked around the room. She looked at her brother.

"Well," she sighed, "I was sound
asleep in my nice, neat room. Then, a
gigantic elephant came out of my closet.
That elephant swung his trunk around and
around. He pulled everything off my
shelves and out of my drawers and toy
chest. Didn't you hear his angry, honking
noise? I was so scared that I stayed right
in my bed."

Woo Jong looked at Jung Soo. He looked all around the room, and then he said, "Yes, I <u>did</u> hear a honking noise. You must have been very frightened! It is too bad that the elephant did not use his trunk to help you put this room back in order. Now, you will have to do it all by yourself! After you have put your room in order, eaten your breakfast, and come back from the library, you can go with me to see my friend's new kittens." Woo Jong shut the door and went away.

"New kittens! Maybe I can have one!" cried Jung Soo. She jumped out of bed and landed on a pile of dress-up clothes. She shoved the clothes and most of her toys, dolls, and stuffed animals under her bed. Next, she piled the books, puzzles, and games in her toy chest and put her shoes on her shelves. Then, Jung Soo

dumped her blocks into her underwear
drawer. She scooped stuff off the floor and
scattered it on her bed. Then, she pulled
the blanket over it. Jung Soo looked
around her room. Everything was off the
floor. Now, she could go to breakfast! Just
then, someone knocked on the door.
"Come in," said Jung Soo.

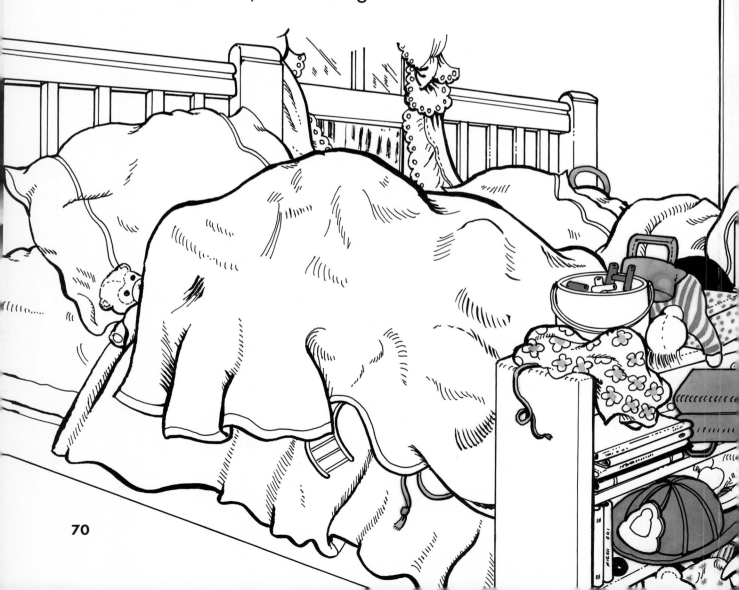

Grandmother poked her head in the door. She looked around the room. She looked at Jung Soo. Then, she asked, "Why are you so late for breakfast?"

Jung Soo answered, "Mother told me to put my room in order before I came to breakfast. Now, I am finished. I am ready for my breakfast!" Jung Soo started out the door.

71

"Wait," said Grandmother. "Show me
how you put your room in order." Jung
Soo showed her everything that she had
done. Grandmother shook her head. "Jung
Soo, tell me where you usually put
everything. I will help you put your room
in order."

Jung Soo and her grandmother sorted her toys and put them away. With Grandmother's help, it didn't take very long. They looked around the room. Everything was organized. Jung Soo's room was back in order. Grandmother smiled and said, "Now, the books, games, and puzzles are on the shelves, your shoes are in the closet, the toys are in your toy chest, the blocks are in your block bag, and the dolls and stuffed animals are on your bed. But tell me, Jung Soo, <u>where</u> did you put the giant, the tornado, and the elephant?"

DRESS-UP

Jung Soo laughed and gave her
grandmother a hug. Then, they went to
breakfast.

Looking for Order

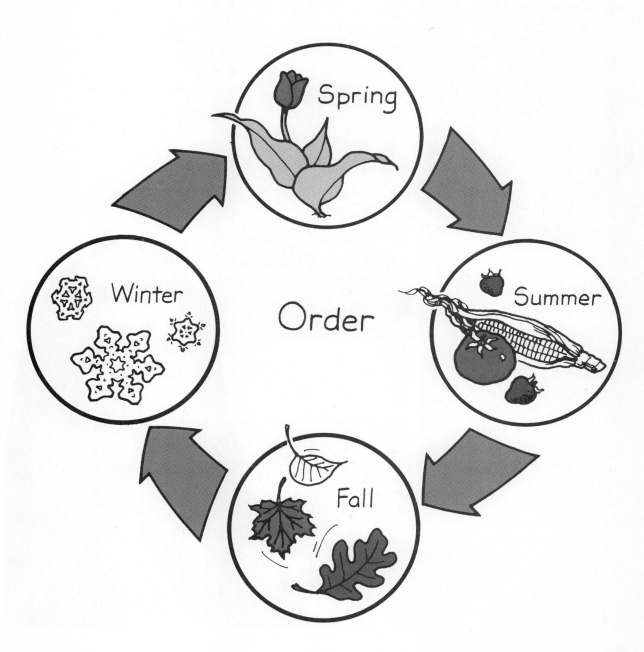

Spring

Summer

Order

Fall

Winter

How do these pictures show order?

How do these pictures show order?

Take Me to the Toy Store

How is this toy store organized?

How are these drawings of animals organized?

Which objects are not in order?

UNIT 3

Materials and Structures

ORDER AND ORGANIZATION IN TECHNOLOGY

Team Skill

Tell others when they do a job well.

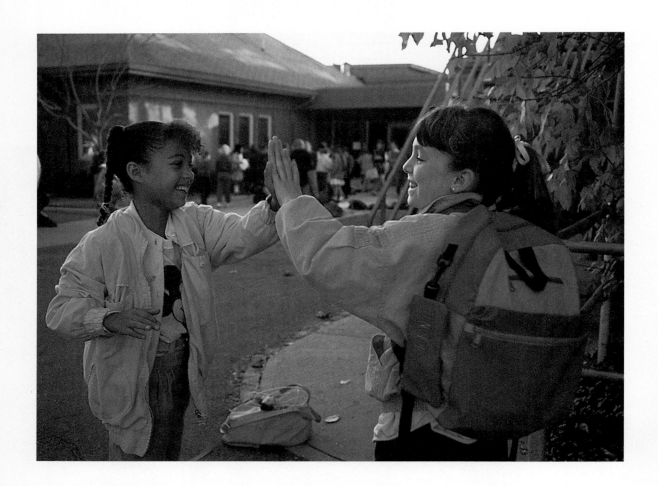

I'll Huff and I'll Puff

The three pigs need help. They need to build houses that the wolf cannot blow down. What things could they use to build their houses?

Make a puffing machine for your team. Use it to test things for the pigs.

You need these things:

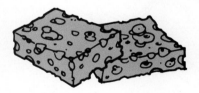

2 sponges

1 straw

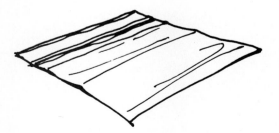

1 plastic bag

2 pieces of tape

A Puffing Machine

Make it like this:

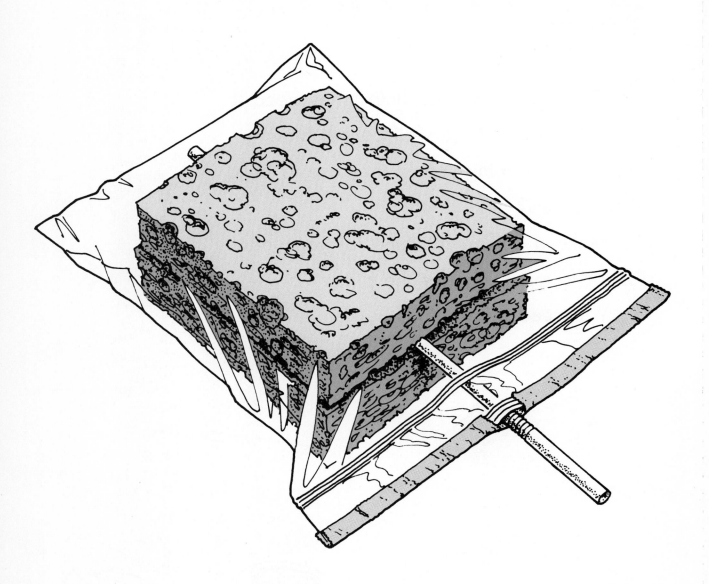

Dear Pigs,

Use these:

These things did <u>not</u> move when we tested them with our puffing machines.

Do not use these:

These things <u>did</u> move when we tested them with our puffing machines.

Your friends,

_____ and _____

Let It Soak In

Wet Pet

The rain fell down,

And soaked my favorite pet.

My dog shook himself,

And now we're both SOPPING wet!

Raindrops, water drops,
From sky to dog to me,
Where's the water now?
Where could it be?

Name _____

The Drop Test

Which things will absorb water? Test them and see.

For our test we will use _____ drops.

To wait, we will count to _____ .

These things <u>do</u> absorb water.

These things <u>do not</u> absorb water.

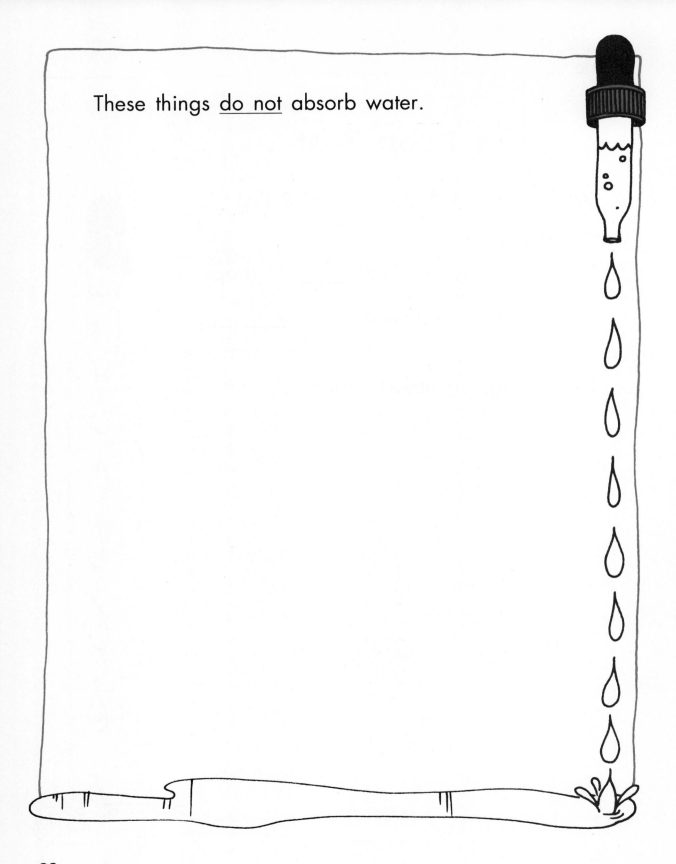

We Think It Will—
We Think It Won't

Some things absorb water, and some things do not. Can you tell which things will or won't absorb water? Your team should draw one picture in each box.

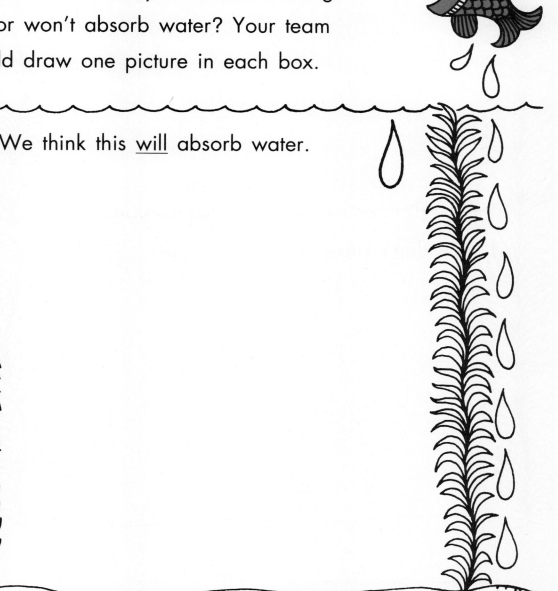

We think this <u>will</u> absorb water.

We think this <u>will not</u> absorb water.

We <u>don't know</u> what this will do.

_____ and _____
     (name)   (name)

I Am Glad

Look around. Find things to draw or
write in both boxes.

I am   these things <u>do</u> absorb water.

I am   these things <u>do not</u> absorb water.

Material Matters

What materials are these objects made of?

Name _____

Looking for Materials

Look around. Find objects to draw or
write in each box.

Materials are
everywhere!

Some objects are made of <u>one</u> material.

Some objects are made of <u>more than one</u> material.

Some objects are made of <u>strange</u> materials.

What Is Happening Here?

106

Why aren't gloves made of glass?

The Book Nook

Silly Store

GRAND OPENING

THE BOOK NOOK
BOOKS FOR CHILDREN OF ALL AGES

OPEN

Put It in This

What do you store or keep in these structures?

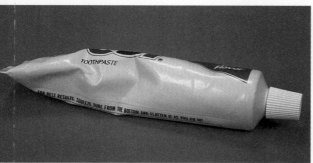

Put It in This

Beds for Bears

The Three Bears

How are these structures alike and different?

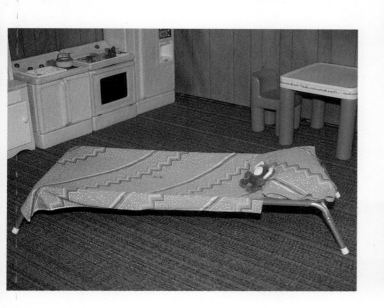

Puffy Pig

Puffy Pig Says

I'm as safe as safe can be.

A puffing machine won't worry me.

It can huff and puff,

But not hard enough.

My structure is PUFFPROOF,

Don't you see?

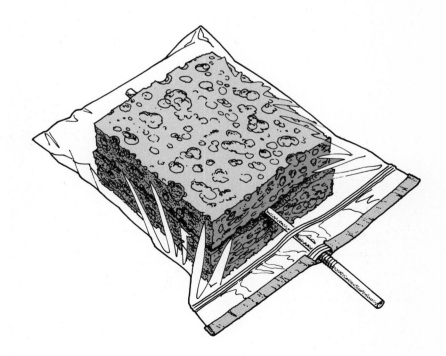

I'm as dry as dry can be.

A water dropper won't worry me.

It can drop more drops,

I don't care if it stops!

My structure is WATERPROOF,

Don't you see?

A Puffproof, Waterproof Structure

Tell another team about your structure.
Talk about these things:

1. What materials did you use?

2. Why did you choose these materials?

3. How did you put the materials together?

4. What happened when you tested your structure?

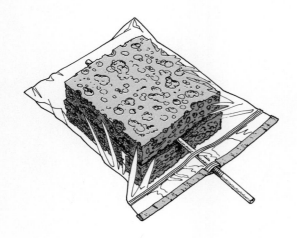

UNIT 4

Safety and Security
ORDER AND ORGANIZATION IN HEALTH

Rules or No Rules?

Rules You Know

What rules do you know about this?

What rules do you know about this?

What rules do you know about this?

What rules do you know about this?

What rules do you know about this?

What rules do you know about this?

What rules do you know about this?

What rules do you know about this?

What rules do you know about this?

What rules do you know about this?

What rules do you know about this?

What rules do you know about this?

What rules do you know about this?

What rules do you know about this?

What rules do you know about this?

What rules do you know about this?

What rules do you know about this?

Team Skill

Ask for help and give help.

Rules for Norule

Rules

Rules are something that

Rules are important because

Be Smart and Safe

Smart and Safe Rules

If there is a fire,

1. Yell "Fire!"

Fire!
Fire!
Fire!

2. Get out!

EXIT →

3. Get help!

| Phone | Grownup | Alarm |

You come home from school. Fire is coming out of the front window. You want to get some things out of your room. What should you do?

You do not go inside. You want to get
help to put out the fire. Where do you go
to get help?

You wake up and smell smoke. It is dark so you turn on the light. You see smoke. You are afraid. What should you do?

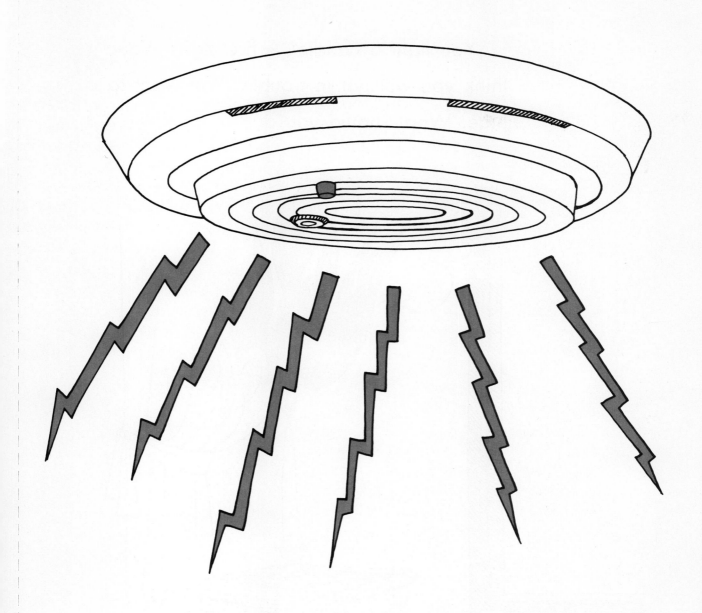

You wake up. You hear the smoke
alarm. You want to go back to sleep.
What should you do?

You light a candle. A fire starts. You think you will get in trouble. You want to hide. What should you do?

Stop, Drop, and Roll

Smart and Safe Rules

If your clothes are on fire,

stop,

drop,

roll.

Drop

Stop

Buckle Up

Busy Bucklebear*
Zips everywhere,
In a zippy car.

Smart, safe Bucklebear
Buckles up with care,
Whether it's near or far.

* The character "Bucklebear," used here by permission, is
copyrighted by Weiner/Seaman Productions, Glendale, California.

 Bucklebear says, "Buckle up!"

Who?

When?

Why?

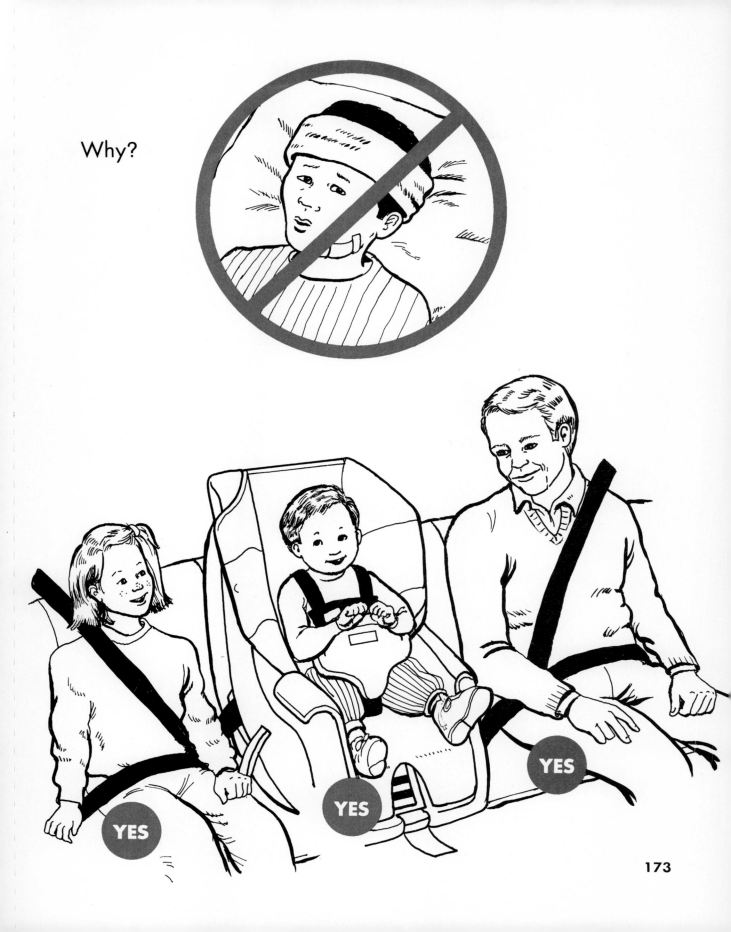

YES

YES

YES

Buckle-up Tag

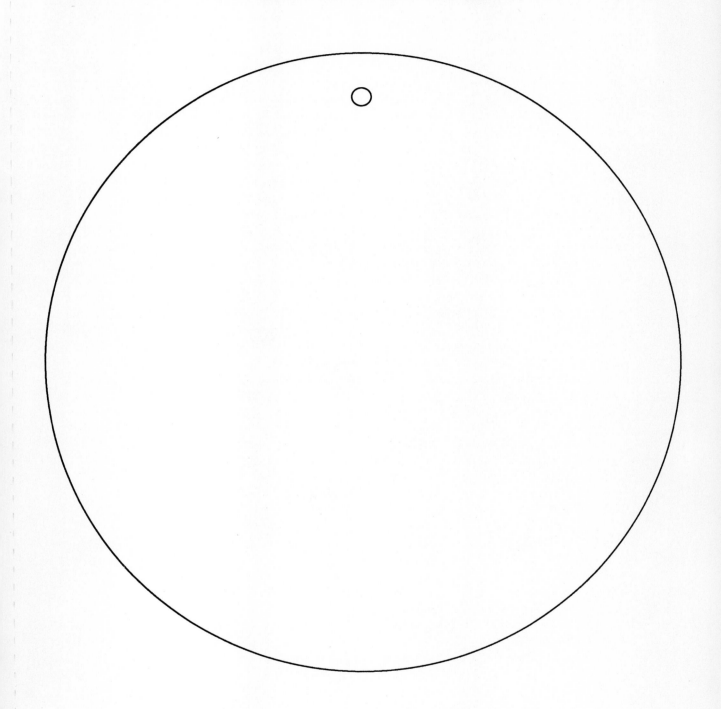

Safe Choices

Safety Rules

Write a safety rule to use to keep out
of danger.

Write a safety rule to use in a burning building.

Safety Rules

Write a safety rule to use if your clothes catch on fire.

Write the most important safety rule for riding in a car.

All Mixed Up

Feelings Wheel

How do you feel?

Your team will make two feelings wheels to show feelings.

You need your book and these things:

2 paper plates

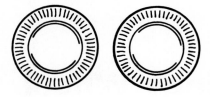

2 pairs of scissors

2 paper fasteners

2 pointers

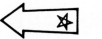

glue

Tear out this page.

Read the next pages to find out what
to do.

Faces Circle

For each feelings wheel, do these things:

1. Cut out the faces circle.

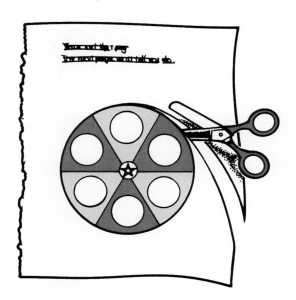

2. Glue it on top of a paper plate.

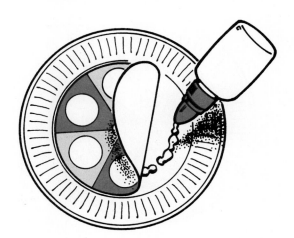

3. Cut out the pointer.

4. Put the star on the pointer on top of
   the star on the faces circle.

5. Push the fastener through both stars.
   Be careful not to poke your finger.

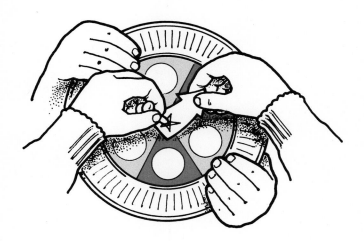

6. Fold back the ends of the fastener.

 # No! Stop!

Smart and Safe Rules

If someone makes you feel confused or bad,

say "No!"

get away,

tell.

Finger Puppets

Finger puppets are fun to make. You just need your finger and a marker.

Will your finger puppet's voice sound like yours, or will it sound like someone else's?

What's Okay?

What's Okay?

Should I use the rules?

Sample	Yes	No
1.	Yes	No
2.	Yes	No
3.	Yes	No
4.	Yes	No

Name _____

1. How would you tell someone to stop bothering you? Write the words.

What would you do?

2. Someone bothers you. Who would you tell? Write that person's name, or draw a picture of the person.

ACKNOWLEDGMENTS

Text

Bucklebear is a registered trademark.

Photo

Photo research by Carlye Calvin, Nederland, Colorado.
All photographs, including cover, by Carlye Calvin.

Art

Katy Keck Arnsteen, Susan Banta, Bill Basso, Diane Bronstein, Joe Cabrera, Eulala Conner (Publishers' Graphics), Sally Laffely, Cheryl Kirk Noll, Roz Schanzer (Craven Design)

Editorial, design, and production services provided by
The Book Department, Inc.